CW01064447

NINE DAYS
(17th to 25th September 1944)

The authentic description of a glider pilot's experience
at Arnhem, from take-off to his escape. A graphic,
detailed, and most absorbing account.

by

RONALD GIBSON

late Staff Serjeant
F Squadron, The Glider Pilot Regiment

Illustrated by Gordon C. Power

ISBN: 978-178035-344-9

First published 1956 by Arthur Stockwell Limited,
Torrs Park, Ilfracombe, North Devon, United Kingdom.

This edition published 2012 by Fast Print Publishing,
9 Culley Court, Bakewell Road, Orton Southgate, Peterborough,
United Kingdom.

In 1956, our father, the late Ronald Gibson, published *Nine Days*, an account of his experiences as a glider pilot during the Battle of Arnhem. The book describes in detail the launch of Operation Market Garden on 17 September 1944, his personal recollections of the day-to-day battles with German troops in the Netherlands and the eventual withdrawal of the British forces over the Rhine nine days later.

Ronald served as a Staff Sergeant with the Glider Pilot Regiment in F Squadron, No. 2 Wing. He was one of only 2000 of the 10,000 British Airborne troops who managed to escape over the river to safety. After serving in Europe he was posted to Fatehjang in Pakistan where he finished writing *Nine Days* in June 1945.

Nine Days has been out of print for many years. However, the interest in this famous Second World War military engagement continues to grow, particularly as very few of the men who fought at Arnhem are alive today. This book is being re-published both as a tribute to our father and also to the British soldiers who fought at Arnhem.

Our family is indebted to several people who have helped to bring this second edition to fruition. Thanks must firstly go to Andy Bellwood from Lincolnshire, whose own father, J.J.G Bellwood, also fought at Arnhem, serving with E Squadron, No. 2 Wing. Andy's encouragement, advice and support have been invaluable in ensuring the re-print of *Nine Days*. Also thanks to Joan Power, the widow of Gordon C.Power, who has generously given her permission to re-use the original illustrations from the 1956 edition. Lastly, thanks must go to graphic artist Chris Tonkin who undertook the layout and design for this second edition and who also helped to co-ordinate the printing.

Candy Gibson
on behalf of the Gibson family

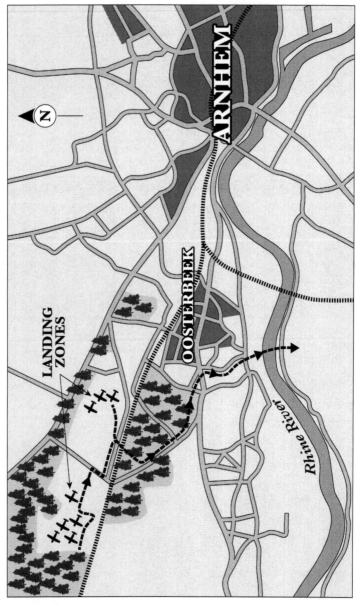

(Route marked thus ▬▬►) Map of Oosterbeek area.

Contents

Day 1 Sunday 17th September, 1944   1

Day 2 Monday 18th September, 1944   17

Day 3 Tuesday 19th September, 1944   29

Day 4 Wednesday 20th September, 1944   37

Day 5 Thursday 21st September, 1944   49

Day 6 Friday 22nd September, 1944   57

Day 7 Saturday 23rd September, 1944   63

Day 8 Sunday 24th September, 1944   71

Day 9 Monday 25th September, 1944   81

DAY 1
Sunday 17ᵗʰ September, 1944

The towmaster waved his green flag. The towplane taxied forwards: its slipstream flicked some gravel on to our windscreen. The rope that lay before us on the concrete writhed into movement: it slowly tautened and lifted clear of the ground: we heard the nosewheel beneath us jar and rumble as we gathered speed. The stones and pine chips and tar beneath us mingled into a grey blur; the towplane lifted its tail: the chequered box, the C.O.'s car, the C.O., the runway crossing, swept past our side. A few seconds later the stones and pine chips and tar floated gently from beneath us. Then the towplane rose from the runway, over the yellow flags, a line of tractors, a steamroller, a picketed glider, over the boundary fence and the walls of a farm.

In the cabin of the Horsa we carried a six pounder gun and the jeep that would tow it into action. In the rear seats sat two men of the Border Regt., the driver and the gunlayer. Our route led from Base to Arnhem, by way of Aldeburgh on the Suffolk coast. The maps for this route were lying on the cockpit floor, crumpled layers of white with red and blue and green markings, pencil lines scribbled from point to point. At this moment they were being folded in the hands of Sim.

"Sim" was my co-pilot. He was a German Jew from Berlin, a refugee who had arrived in England a few months before the declaration of war. I had only known him a few weeks. He was small and dark and very thin, with the finely chiselled features found among intelligent Jews. I knew very little about him. While we were waiting on the towpath a few minutes before he had recalled the first incidents of his life I had heard him mention: a drift from post to post; a brief engagement to a girl, broken by his flight from Germany.

After passing the farmyard we flew into some low lying mist. The landscape lay before us in dim layers of morning sky, sour green meadow and the swathes of mist below. On our starboard we passed the town of Fairford, with its church and millrace and the park and the glassy lake. We flew low, at three hundred feet in a wide circle that led us back over the airfield. On the turn we passed the black railyards and streets of Swindon. I began to sweat beneath my clothes: we were dressed in full battle order, with heavy cloth smocks over our tunics. At Cirencester I handed the controls over to "Sim". The Dakota began to climb.

We crossed the airfield at 800 feet. The mist had lifted slightly and we could see the broad plateau with its surround of beechwoods, its intricate pattern of runway sand perimeter track, the hangers and neat rows of nissen huts like lines of excavated tube stations.

The Dakota turned on to the course for Aldeburgh. We passed Bampton church spire, the old canal, the water meadows with their lines of willows and rush beds, and flew between the two channels of the Thames.

A cloud crossed the sun: the fields darkened and the streams and dykes turned from dark brown to silver grey. We vanished into the base of a cloud, and the Dakota towed us down to where the air was clearer, skimming the crest of a hill.

We crossed the Thames at Culham bridge, near a hill cloaked with oaks and bramble heath. We crossed it again by the playing fields, near the old observatory with the hexagonal tower, the gasometers and the Woodstock road. At this point our tug pilot saw a gap in the cloud: he towed us higher through the cloud fringes, where damp streamers curled past the windscreen, parting to reveal a grey green Dakota in a halo of sky, closing and opening again and again. At two thousand feet we rose into clear air.

For the first time since we set off I could see the entire column of tugs and gliders receding into the distance before me. Those furthest ahead had shrunk to midget size, like insects impaled on the blanket of cloud. The morning sun lay still low on our side, and cast long blue shadows from the higher billows of cloud across the lower carpet. We saw a second train of tugs and gliders approaching from the Berkshire Downs. The air was very still, and inside our cockpit we felt we were hanging motionless, while nothing moved but the wisps of cloud that flicked past the window.

Over Wendover the lower clouds dissolved and the green and brown and yellow patchwork of the Chilterns lay spread beneath. Over Ashridge park I sensed the same mood of unreality that I had felt when we passed the home airfield. I had walked and cycled over Ashridge park as a schoolboy. Now, I was a native paying a fleeting return, divided by a curtain of air two thousand feet thick, detached and so very remote. At this moment "Sim" handed back the controls and sat back to munch a biscuit.

At this height the air turned colder and our legs grew numb. I asked "Sim" to draw some hot tea from the Thermos flask. This was one of the luxuries of flying, when one could lean back in the seat, sipping at the slippery rim of the cup, and watch the other man sweat at the wheel.

A few minutes later we saw one of the leading gliders cast off and turn back beneath us. It circled over a wood and headed for the aerodrome at Hatfield. In a moment it vanished behind the edge of the perspex. We heard later that the tug pilot had ordered it to release when his plane failed in one engine.

Over Hertford we met some high cumulus. The towplane flew straight into them: I pushed the controls forward to bring the Horsa below the slipstream. This position had to be assumed when one flew in dense cloud.

"Sim" tried without success to call the tug pilot over the telephone: it had broken down, a not infrequent occurrence. The pointers on the blind tow indicator jerked from side to side. The cable dragged away to one side, when to our good fortune the clouds parted and we flew into the clear.

The Essex fields were mottled by the giant shadows of cloud. The bomber stations of East Anglia slid below and behind, one by one, into green vacancy. We passed the Ispwich estuary, the mud flats and wharves, the forest of cranes and chimney stacks.

It was midday when we reached the coast at Aldeburgh. "Sim" was sitting at the controls. I crawled back along the fuselage over the gun and trailer to carry a mugful of tea to the Borderers in the rear seats. Through a porthole I glimpsed a waste of heath, a streak of dappled sands and the pale shallows of the North Sea. I passed the mug through a gap between the trailer and the plywood roof: it was grasped by the gunlayer.

The two Borderers looked cheerful enough. One was a corporal, short and dark, who lived in Birmingham: the other was a taller, fair north countryman from Tyneside. We had met them on the towpath only twenty minutes before we left: we had shaken hands, chatted for a few minutes and smoked each others cigarettes. From forty minutes after our landing I never saw them again.

When I returned to the cockpit we had left the coast far behind. Another Horsa had just cast off and was drifting down towards the wrinkled sea. I craned over the sill of the windscreen to watch it ditch on the water: it floated over a shallow reach where the sand gleamed pink and yellow beneath the sea: it vanished behind the plywood.

Over the water the air was very still. Where the sea below was stilled in the deeper reaches the darker blue of the water seemed but a darker sky, till the illusion was broken by the foamy wake of a launch or the smoke trail from a steamer.

We sighted the Dutch coast at a quarter to one. Our first glimpse was of a brown blur in the haze below the horizon. It changed to a hard line of white beach and tawny dunes of sand and gorse. I wondered what "Sim" was thinking. I felt the same coldness, a vacuum of emotion, a sense of fatality that I supposed all people felt in moments of crisis. We heard the thud of exploding flak: two black smudges burst above the cloud.

Over the land the cloud wisps floated a little lower. When a couple of shells burst close above the towplane, the pilot wheeled to starboard and towed us into the heart of a dense cumulus. All but a dozen feet of the rope was shrouded in vapour. We tried to dive down into the blind flying position, but the rope sagged lower though "Sim" was pushing at the stick. A second later we emerged from the cloud to see the tug a hundred feet below, half hidden beneath our nose. The rope tautened with a jerk.

Looking at the map, we found the land beneath us was Schouwen Island; it was divided from the mainland by a narrow channel. The Germans had breached the sea dykes and all we could see were narrow banks between the lakes of grey water, a few trees and tiled roofs, a church spire and several windmills. On our port side lay the Maas estuary, a tracery of blue channels interlacing between shimmering flats of mud, recently uncovered by the tide. We crossed the channel, a main road, a railway and our first town, a bundle of houses nestling round a tall building with stepped gables. Before us lay Brabant, a network of roads and dykes and polders.

In twenty minutes we reached our first turning point at Hertogenbosch. It looked like a city of the dead, a sprawling toytown that was too neat and new and pink to be real. We had expected a little fire over a town of this size, but none came. A mile past the central square our column turned north-eastward: as we banked round I looked below and saw wave after wave of aircraft slide diagonally beneath us. They were flying on our previous course, heading for Nijmegen and Eindhoven, the landing grounds for the American airborne divisions. A thin fleece of clouds lay between us, rent by gaps of blue.

As we straightened on to our final course this cloudy veil dissolved to reveal a bleak expanse of fields, then scattered pinewoods and an occasional row of poplars. Their shadows here crept inwards almost to nothing. Ahead lay the black line of the Maas.

The Maas was dark and apparently swift, for streaks of spray flecked the water on the bends and in the shallows. On the further bank the land lay bleaker still, empty of house or tree. Five minutes later we crossed the Waal, the main stream of the Rhine, the widest river I had yet seen: it was broad enough for the water to be churned into waves as high as those of the sea. On either side we could trace the shadows of dykes that stemmed the winter floods. Projecting from each bank were quoins of stone and earth, like rows of teeth.

In five minutes we would cross the ploughland by Wolfheze station. One recalled the lamplit vault of the "briefing" hut at Base, its wall hung with maps and plans and photographs, the printed sheets of codes and regiments and their rendezvous. At the far end there had stood a trestle table with a "mosaic" of air photographs pinned across it. A line of red chalk had traced our course over the fields, over two villages, a river bend, a plantation, a railway track, up to a broad arrow over a dark rectangle of ploughland enclosed by a forest of pine and stretches of heath.

The fields, the two villages, the river bend and the plantation came into sight. In the pine plantation I saw a starlike pattern of roads and paths radiating from a high tower. A pall of smoke drifted over the forest and a red circle flamed among the trees beside the railway. The ploughland was framed within a border of tall pines. In the centre fluttered a plume of purple smoke, a signal from the troops who had already landed.

"Are you all right? This is the place." The voice in the earphones trailed off in a crackle. I heard "Sim's" voice answer. "Yes, not so bad. Thanks for the tow. Good-bye." I pulled the release lever and the rope jerked past the window and out of sight.

The roar of wind outside the panes died to a gentle hiss. The sky around was filled with floating gliders. We were flying too high and I pushed the flap lever to the "half down". The Horsa tilted forward, like a sled on the steepening of a slope, and the earth swung up towards us, hiding the sky. We saw a row of trucks on the line, people running, two fires in the wood, and the flash of a bomb bursting on a house. The big fire that we had first seen rose from a long brick building that looked like a hospital, with gutted roof and broken walls. We slewed away to the side of the clearing to lose further height, then turned in towards the furthest field over the gutted roof and a row of oaks. I pushed the lever down to "full flap". We sank like a lift. The field was littered with the leading gliders. We headed for a clearing, screened by the smoke from the flare.

We skidded to a standstill about fifty yards from the edge of the woods. The Borderers banged open the rear door and jumped out. We followed. The sky resounded with the roar of engines; the woods and fields were silent. We each lit a cigarette. Someone picked up an axe handle and hammered at the bolts on the tail. In half an hour the bolts were loose and the tail fell to the earth. We heaved it across the furrows, straining with our backs against the plywood. The corporal started the engine of the jeep, let in the clutch and jerked the gun down the ramp and skidded across the furrows in a cloud of earth. We heaved our rucksacks on to the bonnet and sat ourselves beside. The Borderers carried us to a corner of the wood by the railway embankment. We dumped the rucksacks in the ditch, stepped aside, and waved them goodbye.

Our rendezvous had been placed at this corner. A party of about sixty glider pilots were lying under the trees: others were patrolling the path by the railway. It had been planned that we should rendezvous in squadrons and march off separately towards the town park, where we would dig in for the night.

After our struggle with the tail, "Sim" and I were among the last to arrive in our particular squadron. The others slung their arms and we moved off down a footpath between the embankment and a row of young pines that screened the fields on our left. A few yards down we met an acquaintance named "George". He was escorting three Dutch civilians, a man and two very pretty girls. One of the girls called "Good luck". We replied with some ribald comments on "George's" behaviour with women, and passed on.

A few yards from a level crossing a sniper's bullet whizzed overhead. We jumped off the path and lay flat in the hollow between the ploughed furrows and the turf bank. Two scouts were ordered forward.

At this moment the colonel walked up and ordered us to wait. I lay back, pillowed against my rucksack. "Sim" began talking to a Dutch boy who had appeared from behind the trees. Two signallers passed us dragging a handcart loaded with a bundle of wire. The scouts returned with our first prisoner. He was a grey-faced little man, dressed in a shabby uniform with a peaked cap. He did not seem frightened – only a little dazed from the interruption of his Sunday afternoon.

We moved on a few yards, then halted again at the end of a long avenue of oak trees. The afternoon sun was drawing low and the trees cast long shadows across the path, in regular file, like the black keys of a piano. A few yards away stood a neat farmhouse, with pink walls and a pantiled roof. A group of men were talking by the wall. Three of them were dressed in civilian clothes, blue trousers, and white shirts, with black armbands marked "Oranje". They were talking to a brigadier and a thin man dressed in khaki and blue, a war correspondent.

Once again we were called to our feet. We turned right at a crossroads, in the direction of the town. Before us lay another tree-lined path that broadened into a road, cobbled in the centre, with earthen pavements. On either side stood a row of little houses, each in its own flower garden and allotment. The sun filtered through the trees of a copse.

At every garden gate there was gathered a group of Dutchmen, with their wives and children. Some of them had placed wash tubs and baskets filled with fruit on the pavement, and the children were running forwards with apples. At one gate stood an old man in a blue cap, who saluted each party as it passed.

Suddenly we heard the loud crack of a gun and a cloud of earth burst upwards from the pavement. We dived headlong for the bank of mould at the foot of the trees. A second or so later the cloud dissolved. The road lay clear in front, but the groups had vanished from the garden gates: there was a gaping hole in a fence: some glass tickled from a broken window as the wind blew a sudden gust.

A Recce corps cyclist pedalled back along the road. He told us that the shell had come from a German armoured car as it crossed the road junction a hundred yards ahead.

Our section officer ordered us to move into the side gardens and place ourselves under cover near to the back palings. We were to watch the open fields.

I lay down behind a hump of earth beside a woodshed. I was joined by Gordon, the man behind me in the column. We peered forward through a screen of grass and nettles over a field where some dappled cows and a carthorse were cropping the grass. A chilly silence had followed the crack of the gun and we could hear the sound of their munching. I felt a hand touch my shoulder. I turned to see the old, blue-capped Dutchman standing with a jug of milk in one hand and a cup in the other. He placed them on the ground beside us and pointed to the corner of his house, where a ragged gap showed in the brickwork, the mark of Allied bombing. "Nix," he said, "you here, we free." A day or two later these words would be tinged with irony.

I thought what a farcical war this was. There were we, crouching behind cover in the garden, waiting for the enemy to show his head, while an old man was pottering about, quite unconcerned, attending to our comfort. I had seen a similar instance in Normandy: a crowded village street, with British infantry filing along the shadow of a wall, trailing a German sniper who was hiding in the churchyard, while old women hobbled over the stones with baskets under their arms on the way to the baker's shop.

We waited for half an hour, while Bren carriers rumbled down the road and cyclists pedalled to and fro. Two jeeps drove back loaded with casualties. These were perched on stretchers lashed to the awning frames.

The old man brought us a bowl of plums. This time he took more care to avoid revealing our position: he crawled round the corner of the woodshed.

A voice recalled us to the road. Major M ----- was giving our flight commander his final orders. We were to move forward to a plantation of pines a quarter of a mile past Wolfheze station.

We shouldered our packs and marched forward in file. At the roads we turned right and approached the station. On our left stood the charred shell of the building we had glided past on our approach to land.

An anti-tank gun was mounted beside the gate post, pointing down the road towards a level crossing. A broken cycle lay in the ditch beside a dead German. A group of gunners were sitting on the gunpit wall. We smelt a whiff of cordite.

We turned left at the railway embankment and stumbled down a narrow path in some heather. The heather bells dusted our anklets. We heard a continuous crackle of Bren fire from the wood in front.

Some bullets whistled over the embankment and flickered into the heather. We lay flat and watched the wood. Presently the firing stopped: after a short silence we heard two or three spasmodic bursts, then a further silence. We rose and moved down into the trees.

The young pines stood in serried ranks. Their branches interlocked overhead and cast a deep continuous shadow through the wood. On the further side we could see the glimmer of dusk through the trunks. A section of the Recce corps walked past us towards the path we had trod. It was their fire we had heard when we lay in the heather.

When the column had halted Major M---- called the flight commander to one side. We leaned on our rifles and waited. Lieut W ---- returned and told us the area our squadron had to hold: it was a square portion of the wood at its southern end, bordered on three sides by open heath, on the fourth by a narrow path. He walked with us over the western edge of the trees, a few yards within the shadow, and showed us where to dig.

I chose a level patch between two trees and stacked my rucksack and rifle against a trunk. I saw that Gordon had begun to dig his foxhole a few yards to the right. It gave one comfort to dig down into needles and sand. When we first halted I had felt too tired to move, until I remembered the cycle and the dead body on the road.

I had parted company from "Sim" after we had scattered from the shell in the roadway by the old Dutchman's house. I saw him digging with another section at the corner by the path. I never realised that in three days time I would never see him again.

DAY 2
Monday 18th September, 1944

Throughout the night we staged a patrol of six men, divided into hourly shifts, with two parties patrolling down the sides of the wood and meeting at the corners for a whispered conference. Gordon and I formed one such party, with another pilot whose name I have forgotten. We paced back and forth down the path listening to the sound of distant firing and the nearby crackle of twigs. At intervals of fifteen minutes we met the other three at the north-east corner. There we squatted in the heather and scanned a broad waste of heath where a line of gorse was blazing. At thirty minutes past the hour we met at the south-west corner, at the intersection of two paths below the railway embankment, one of them a broad track that followed the line of the railway.

On the far side of this track we could see a vague white shape like a giant fungus. It was the bared chest of a dead sergeant: his body had been laid ready for the morning burial. He belonged to the Recce party we had met as we entered the wood at dusk.

When our shift ended I wrapped myself in a gas cape and blanket and lay in my foxhole. The noise of firing continued till dawn. The wind chilled my back and I passed a sleepless night.

A few minutes after daybreak Major M --- walked round to inspect the position. The last shift of the guard returned to their trenches. I heard the morning orders as they were passed to the section commanders. Weapons would be cleaned and our kit packed ready for a quick advance: rations could be opened. I opened my box and lit the hexamine cooker in the hollow in the ground. This cooker was a neat device, a tin tripod that folded into a pocket, holding a tablet of hexamine the size and shape of a can of boot polish. The ration boxes held a day's portion of oatmeal and biscuit, some sugar, tea, and sweets, and a cube of meat extract that tasted like spiced sawdust.

After breakfast Lieut. W ---- told Gordon and me that we were to join his patrol. He had been told to scout eastwards along the embankment path and then to return in a wide circle across the open heath.

We assembled at the side of the path, and set off in line, Gordon and myself were placed as leading scouts. A hundred yards down the path we saw a derelict car standing opposite the mouth of a tunnel. As we approached we heard a scuffling sound inside the cab and a low groaning.

At this moment a figure in a blue overcoat bobbed up from the tunnel mouth. My right eardrum was almost split by a clanging burst from the Bren gun.

"It's a civvy," said Lieut W ---. "Hold it. Let him come out."

A voice called from the tunnel. In a nervous moment the Bren gunner fired another shot. The round spattered against the brick arch and whizzed into the grass. Someone ran back down the tunnel. The steps faded into silence.

We watched the entrance, while W ---- walked forward and peered into the car. We heard him murmur a few words. The groaning stopped and we heard a faint answer. W ---- turned from the car and moved over to the tunnel mouth. He stood for a moment in the entrance, waved his hands in front as a signal that all was clear, then returned to where we lay.

"There's a Recce trooper in the back seat. Badly hit. Got caught in an ambush last night. One of their sergeants was killed."

I remembered the body we had seen on the patrol.

On the far side of the car stood an abandoned jeep. We pulled the trooper from his seat and laid him in the American truck. Someone started the engine. The rest of us ran back and lay in the long grass. The driver backed into the path, turned and vanished up the slope in a cloud of sand and smoke.

W ---- motioned us to rise. At this moment a Bren carrier rattled down the path. Beside the driver stood a slim captain of the Recce corps, wearing spectacles and a camouflage net tied pirate fashion round his head. The carrier stopped. W ---- walked over to him and told him the story of the trooper and the ambush.

The captain offered to drive forward up the ridge in front and cover the advance of our patrol. A copse of young pines stood on the crest: they grew close enough to shelter an ambush. It was probable that the enemy had used them so the night before. The carrier lurched forward, mounted the slope and disappeared among the trees. A minute later it returned to the path. He reported that the copse was empty.

We moved northwards across the heath. I resumed my place as leading scout with Gordon pacing twenty yards distant on the right flank. For three or four hundred yards we moved across open ground. I felt as naked as Adam striding alone through the heather and cursed my luck at being placed in the lead.

We turned westwards at a path that led towards the northern boundary of our wood. When we had arrived at the corner of the fence we closed together and returned to camp in file under cover of the trees.

The remainder of the squadron had donned their equipment: they were awaiting the order to advance. W --- told Gordon and me that we were to remain behind as a rear party: our task was to act as guides to the second half of the squadron when they arrived in the afternoon with the second day's lift of troops and supplies.

When the main party had moved away Gordon and I sat down on the bank of an empty trench. The position looked like a ravaged cemetery, with the foxholes for graves. We walked down to the corner by the embankment and chose a long trench from where we could obtain a clear view of the path. We heard some mortar shells falling on the far side of the railway.

For the next two days, now "Sim" had been moved to another section, Gordon became my constant companion. There are curious friendships made in wartime: close but short in duration, broken by parting, never to be resumed, though the partners may re-encounter in some company only a few weeks later. I had known Gordon in an off-hand fashion for a whole year, but never intimately.

He was a short, pale, clerical-looking man with hair thinning at the temples. He had been trained in the infantry: I believe in the South Staffordshires. He retained the inherent smartness of an infantryman: as an individual he was independent, home-loving and a little contemptuous of military standards.

When the mortar fire had ceased we moved out to a sunlit corner of the wood and rested on the carpet of pine-needles. At the crossing of the path by the railway we could see the grave of the Recce sergeant, a leaf strewn mound topped by a cross of newly cut branches: a paper strip inscribed with his name and unit flapped in the wind. On the crest of the embankment the polished steel of the rails shimmered in the heat. Occasionally we saw a patrol cross the skyline. It was hard to distinguish whether they were British or German: later we learnt to detect the German helmet by its polished glitter, devoid of grit, paint, or camouflage. From the sky we heard the continuous hum of distant planes.

The gliders landed at three o'clock. They were heralded by long, crackling bursts of flak from some German batteries a few miles to the north. The lower sky was blurred by a haze of smoke that billowed from the flares our troops had lit on the landing zone. Our position lay beneath the final corner of the glider's circuit: we could hear the low hiss of their passage through the air. They flew in a long, straggling line, scattered by the shells that burst in their path: we counted them in clusters of two or three. The barrage increased in sound. They began to dive at greater speed, striving to gain the shelter of the trees before they levelled out to skim the furrows.

For several Horsas this added speed courted disaster. From where I stood the landing zone was concealed by a line of poplars on the far side of an allotment. I saw a glider dive for a gap between the trees and turn to clear a branch with his wing-tip. The wing struck and snapped in two. I heard a heavy thump and the splintering of plywood. Another soared in downwind, its nose struck the field and it bounced fifty feet into the air, stalling on the treetops fifty yards from our position.

They were using another landing zone on the far side of the railway on a wide carpet of heath and field extending to the river. We saw a flight of Hamilcars wheel and vanish below the skyline of the bank.

The sky was patterned by a multitude of planes. Within half an hour three hundred gliders must have landed. The towplanes circled westward, trailing tentacles of rope. A thousand feet above a screen of fighters wreathed their arabesques among the wisps of cloud. They flew in waves, the hum of engines rose and fell in volume, gradually to fade and cease. The sky cleared.

I ran northwards through the woods to where I had seen the Horsa fall on the trees. I found it, couched on a bed of splintered trunks, its wings splintered at the root, one splayed back against the trunk of a thick pine. The nose had crumpled inwards as if it were cardboard. I looked for the pilot.

He was standing among a group of his passengers, three of them were medical orderlies. He was grazed slightly on the forehead, but appeared unshaken. The second pilot was slightly injured, the remainder had escaped unscathed. A party of them were heaving bundles of medicine and bandages from the rear door of the fuselage. I helped them clear the last bundles before I returned to Gordon.

Before my return the second half of our squadron had already assembled. We led them down the path by the railway, past the derelict car and the tunnel mouth. On the further ridge we were met by a runner who led us to the new squadron position.

We found them digging trenches along the edge of a deep copse of silver birch and evergreen. Across our front extended a flat of heather, bounded on the far side by woods. The clearing was littered with an array of parachutes, red and blue and black and yellow: beside them lay the wicker panniers and cylinders in which the supplies had been stored. Parties of men darted from one bundle to the next, seizing all they could hold before the enemy snipers fired too close. The woods around resounded with the crackle of rifle fire. The far side was held by the enemy: they were strafing the ground with two machine guns.

We reported to W ---, our section leader: he was leaning against a tree, munching chocolate. He waved us towards a gap in the bushes and told us to dig.

Within twenty minutes the order was given to move position. This riled me a little, for I had just cleared the topsoil of roots and gravel. We formed into threes and retraced our route down the wood to the railway track. I leaned forward to ease the dull pain in my back, born of a day's hacking and digging and the rub of the pack on my spine. We filed into the tunnel mouth.

We marched for three miles. I remember little of the journey, only a few incidents, vague and disconnected: our passage through the low vault of brick, damp and cold: the clearing where we rested: a pathway through monotonous rows of pine: a dead German at a crossing of the path, who lay like a fallen statue, with frozen limbs and blue-grey face and gaping mouth: the road that led into the town – a very English, suburban road, half paved, half wilderness.

We passed several double gates and gravel drives lined with bushes: the ridge of tiled roofs showed above. The road widened into a street. We halted again beside a park railing, beneath an unlit lamp.

A long line of lorries and guns paraded past in the darkness. They were driven without lights and moved at a funereal pace. Beside the convoy moved a seemingly endless column of men. We heard the echo of tramping feet and the clink of spades from digging parties in the park.

The sound of firing came from all sides: the staccato burst from Spandau and Bren: the sibilant whine of mortar shells: the distant thud of a bomb. The sky was laced with scarlet streaks of tracer and glowed from the reflection of a fire. At the street corners stood groups of men and women, some chattering, others silent and glum.

We sat for several minutes by the railing. The sweat began to chill on my back. Then the order came to move. We turned a corner and marched up a winding lane to the edge of a wood beside a field of stubble. An isolated copse and the gable of a roof were silhouetted against the northern sky. Our section extended in a line along the grass fringe between the stubble and a row of young beeches. We stacked our rucksacks and crawled into cover in a slight depression of the ground screened by the leaves. A guard of two men was posted, we arranged the reliefs among ourselves: then the rest lay down to sleep.

I never slept, but only dozed, for the second night in succession. In the copse across the field we could hear a continuous duel of rifle fire from opposite patrols. Tracer bullets spattered over the stubble and ricocheted in all directions. Occasionally a machine gun would sweep the front of our wood at shoulder height. When my watch had finished I crawled further into the trees and lay behind the sheltering roots of an oak.

Landing at Wolfheze, 17th September 1944

DAY 3
Tuesday 19th September, 1944

Tuesday was a quiet day.

When light returned I began to dig. It was a relief to move again after huddling against the roots of the tree in a vain attempt to gain shelter from the night wind. I chose a patch of ground beneath the low branches of a beech, screened from the field by a line of fern. The soil was moist and sandy: I had cleared a depth of two feet before I halted for breakfast.

Gordon and I shared the labours of cooking. He boiled a tinful while I prepared the tea and biscuits. My method of making tea would have made a housewife weep. We carried it in little cubes of tea, sugar, and milk mixed in powdered form and compressed into a solid: these were dropped into a mess-tin of boiling water, producing a curdled mass of greenish grey liquid that slowly turned to brown. Tea is a much abused drink, regarded in some quarters as "wash". I have always ignored such opinions: I believe the war was won on tea. Later in the week I obtained a whole tinful of this nectar, and brewed my canfuls five or six times a day.

By day the wood wore a friendly air. Behind our line of trenches lay a little path, with a grove of "Christmas tree" firs on the other side: beyond them a lane, bordered with tall conifers, led slantwise through the wood to the eastern edge; beyond lay the inner wood of oaks and beech and pine, receding into shadow.

Thoughout the day green-clad figures hurried to and fro along the path. From one or two of them we gathered our first scraps of news. On the first day the paratroops had advanced straight through the town as far as the river bridge. They had entrenched themselves in a house close to one end of the bridge and were said to be holding out against all attacks. Another force had advanced to Renkum but had been compelled to withdraw. Throughout the previous day the other paratroops and infantry had been striving to break through towards the party at the bridge. It was rumoured that the Second Army had reached Nijmegen and linked up with the Americans.

By midday I had dug a magnificent pit, as large as a grave; six feet by three by six in depth; there was a firing platform at one end and a little niche in one side where I stored my food and ammunition.

After lunch we took turns in drawing water from a cottage at the corner of the wood. It was built of brick and pantiles, enclosed in a garden so compact that it was filled by a row of beans, a flower bed, and a hutch full of tame rabbits. The woman in the kitchen spoke a few words of English. She asked us to fill our pockets with some pears that lay in a bucket by the door.

A troop of field guns were stationed in the field. They blazed away throughout the morning: orders were bellowed through a megaphone and the wireless crackled in the command post. It was a comfort to hear the crack and thud of the charge, to see the sheet of flame belch from the muzzle, and smell the acrid fumes of cordite.

In the afternoon I built a little fire of twigs to boil some water for a wash. Gordon and I sat beside it and peeled off our clothes. Someone walked up and took a photograph.

The third lift arrived at three o'clock. We saw no gliders land, for we had marched several miles on the previous evening and the landing zone was out of sight: but our trenches lay beneath the path of the supply planes which dropped the canisters of arms and ammunition.

They were heralded by a flight of Spitfires that flashed past a few feet above the trees. They vanished over the hill in a few seconds; their high-pitched whine still sang in our ears. Then the flak burst above us in a myriad puff of black smoke. Some splinters of shell spattered through the leaves. A straggling column of Stirlings and Dakotas flew into the puffs of smoke, unswerving in their course. In the narrow segment of sky I saw five of them dive below the hill with engines aflame. From their open bellies streamed a trail of coloured parachutes with panniers dangling from the cords. I saw one Dakota, one engine belching a cloud of smoke, circle three times among the flak before it disgorged its load of canisters.

The panniers and canisters were dragged into the shelter of the wood. Gordon and I retrieved a basket of mortar shells and carried it to a group of Service Corps who waited by a jeep. Some of the canisters had to be dragged down from the upper branches of trees where they had been dropped wide of the field. One case exploded before it was touched; luckily no one was standing nearby.

The planes vanished with the same suddenness that marked their arrival. They were chased by a squadron of Messerschmitts: some of these broke away from the main formation to rake the field with cannon fire.

At five o'clock we moved position. I left my pit with some regret, as though I were a pauper tenant evicted from his ancestral home. It had been fashioned with labour and not a little love. I had to dig four or five of these foxholes before our stay ended: for them all I felt a sneaking form of attachment.

We gathered into a column and behind the flight commander, Captain R ---, we filed out from the wood past the cottage with the rabbit hutch, across a road and down another road, westwards into Oosterbeek.

The road was flanked by houses built in pairs: low cut hedges were entwined round wire fences, enclosing beds of autumn flowers below the bay windows of the front parlours. The sound of firing had faded into a low rumble, drowned by the tramp of feet from the column in front and the laughing voices of the children on the pavement. The house windows were made of plate glass, without panes: we could see clearly into the rooms where the older people sat and watched us pass. A fair girl in a blue frock waved from a dormer window.

At the end of the street we came to a main road leading east towards the town. In the centre of the road was a tramline: the pavement was bordered by an avenue of beeches. High walls pierced by openings with iron gates enclosed the gardens of a row of houses, a little forlorn in appearance, with tall narrow windows and painted shutters. We turned at the next corner and headed northwards towards the park.

The park was a square of beech wood, enclosed by streets on three sides. It was encircled by a line of iron railings, the only "park like" feature; a cluster of stable buildings stood half hidden in the trees. We pushed through a side gate and trudged across a carpet of damp leaves and twigs and nutshells that crackled underfoot. A civilian by the gate warned us that there were snipers in the houses: the leading section filed round to the flank of the stables and fired a few shots into the empty windows. Nothing stirred. They waited for a minute: then two riflemen crawled through an open window. They returned after a brief search to report that the place was empty.

We extended in a line across the wood and advanced slowly towards the far side, scanning the trees for snipers. The undergrowth was too sparse to conceal a man, but some felled timber had been piled in high stacks where a dozen men might hide in one party. In the waning light the leaves fluttered and shifted: a branch would stir in a gust of wind or wave across the bole of a tree.

Our section crawled across a fence and patrolled down a line of gardens to the railing in the north side. We met a young Dutch boy who ran up to our party, grabbed W --- by the shoulder and pointed towards the street. He gabbled some Dutch, which no one could understand, but from his gestures we understood that a sniper was hiding on one of the roofs.

It was too late to patrol further. We turned back into the darkness of the trees. When we rejoined the squadron they had already dispersed and each man was digging a separate pit under cover of a bank, a few yards within the railing. Our position lay along the northern side. I found myself stationed beside Gordon in a shallow depression of the ground. We both began to dig.

"...a sound of running feet on the road"

DAY 4
Wednesday 20th September, 1944

Wednesday was not a quiet day.

I had dug my foxhole about ten feet from the railing.
Across the street I could see another railing enclosing a
square of allotments. In the centre of these stood a blazing
shed: the glow of its flames flickered on the windows of a
row of houses on the left side. In the allotments stood rows
of climbing plants entwined on a trellis of sticks. On these
were draped some scarlet parachutes that had drifted there
on the wind the previous afternoon.

Throughout the night Gordon and I kept watch, each
for a two hour shift at a time. During my periods of rest I
made a vain attempt to sleep, huddled in a gas cape. The
cold and the noise of firing kept me awake. At short intervals
a five barrel German mortar fired salvoes overhead from a
position further to the north. The shells moaned through
the air: "whooh, whooh, whooh, whooh, whooh" – after
a moment's silence they thumped down somewhere to the
south. Five thumps. When my turn came to watch I peered

across at the pink circle of light around the burning shed and the dim skyline of walls and gables. Every few minutes a line of tracers would sprout from a window on the right of the allotment and span the open ground in a shallow curve, spattering against the roof of a house on the left. I heard the rumble of tanks along a distant street: whether they were British or German I could not tell. The two hour shifts seemed endless. I felt very tired, yet very awake, with a pain burning behind the eyes.

After dawn the firing ceased. I began to deepen my hole. I had to crouch, for a low branch of beech that shielded the position impeded the digging. At eight o'clock I stopped for a meal.

I boiled the breakfast porridge and Gordon made the tea. I considered his brew to be inferior to mine, and commented on the fact. He replied by reviling my porridge. We discovered that we had eaten only half the two day ration in three days. The food was very concentrated and unappetising, so this did not surprise us. My strongest craving was for tea and chewing gum to slake my thirst after the spells of digging.

After breakfast Captain R --- organised a patrol. He mustered half the flight, about twenty men, and vanished up the road on the right of the allotment in the direction of the railway. The purpose of the patrol was to reconnoitre the streets in front.

It was twenty minutes to ten when they started. Lieut. L --- stayed behind in charge of the remainder of us. We returned to our digging, while L --- paced about among the trees, cleaning his revolver with a handkerchief. He was tall and pale, with the face of a young boy.

A few civilians passed along the street. An old man wheeled a load of clothes in a barrow: an old woman ran past on clogged feet: a boy peered through the railings, and seeing me, began to speak, but L --- waved him away. A long silence was broken by the five barrel mortar. The moan of the flying shells changed to a high pitched whine: they burst close behind us in the wood.

At five minutes to ten I had cleared my hole to a depth of four feet. I took a swig from the water bottle and sat down for a rest.

I heard a sound of running feet in the road and the sudden burst of a machine gun close above my head. The strewn earth beside the trench was spattered into the air. The footsteps passed on: a second burst sounded from higher up the pavement.

I called to Gordon. I had heard his spade clinking in the gravel a few minutes before. No one answered. I cocked my rifle and peered over the top of the bank across the road. I pulled the grenades from my pocket and placed them in a row on the edge of the trench.

I heard a scuffle among the pea sticks and some one shouted in German. I glanced over my shoulder and saw L--- standing beside a tree, loading his revolver.

Two figures dashed across a gap between the rows of peas. Someone fired. Three more figures followed the first. We all fired and two of them dropped out of sight. I heard one of them groan. A peak capped head rose from where they had fallen. I fired again and the head vanished. Someone shouted from the garden on the right of the allotment and a door slammed in the house beyond. There was a minute's silence.

The enemy's intention was obvious. They were starting a flanking movement, designed to break through in the orchard on our right. I saw L --- walk down to the Bren gun by the orchard fence and murmur something to the gunner. At that moment I heard a motor cycle approaching down the side street to our right. It halted at the house where the door had slammed. Steps sounded on the pavement. Two voices were shouting in German. I began to hate the sound. No order came from L ---, so I thought it was best to lie quiet and wait.

The next moment a smoke canister landed in the centre of the orchard: one of the trees suddenly crackled into flame and the smoke blew across above our heads. A grenade burst a few yards down the railing. There were more shouts in German. One of us fired from his hole by the orchard fence. I heard a scream and a grenade burst in the orchard. The bullet had struck a German in the stomach as he was swinging his arm to throw: the grenade was lobbed vertically into the air and fell back at his feet. I saw a figure kneeling by the house door. I fired and the figure vanished.

There was another pause. I refilled my magazine and dragged a bandolier from the bottom of the trench and laid it beside the grenades. A volley of shots sounded from up the street on our left. They were attacking there too. I looked at my watch. It was five minutes past ten and there was no sign of Captain R ----.

Five or six grenades burst on the orchard fence. I glanced round and saw a man running from the direction of squadron H.Q. He fell face forward over a bursting grenade. A voice in the orchard was shouting in broken English. "Coom out. Coom out. Surrender." I heard them break through the fence and enter the park.

From the other flank on our left I heard a babel of shouting and rifle shots and falling grenades. The road echoed with running feet. They were breaking through the trenches of the other flight.

I looked round to see what L --- was doing. All I saw was a green-clad body sprawling at the foot of a tree: who it was I could not tell. I called to the Bren group by the fence, but no one moved or spoke. A party of Germans scrambled through the fence and ran behind me into the wood. I stood up for a second and called to Gordon and Sim. No one answered.

There was only one thing left to do. I grabbed two of my grenades, the bandolier, and the rifle, and dashed across an open glade into the stacks of wood.

I ran on, zigzagging among the trees and the fallen logs. Once I stumbled and nearly fell. The noise of shouting faded as I passed further into the wood. I crossed a path by the empty stables and pushed through a hedge into a garden on the southern boundary.

I stood on the gravel drive before an empty house. The shutters hung open and the curtains billowed out in the wind. The five barrel mortar fired over the trees of the park. I sprawled in the shelter of some steps. The shells burst in quick succession down the street.

I walked through the gate onto the pavement and recognised the street as one we had crossed the evening before. The road was now pitted with craters. In the evening the gateways had been filled with groups of people waving their hands: one man had run into the road and taken a photograph. Now the street was empty and forlorn, littered with broken glass and tiles.

I sat down and searched my pockets. All I carried was a rifle, two grenades, and forty rounds. Blanket, groundsheet, small kit, food and water bottle – all had been abandoned with my rucksack in the trench.

I wandered southwards through the gardens, looking for a British uniform. A minute later I came back to the main road. At the far side stood a tall shuttered house with a broken slate roof and gaping windows. The walls were pitted with splinter marks: against one was nailed a Red Cross flag. A few yards from the front door stood a battered jeep.

I dashed across the tramlines and round the back of the jeep. Here I nearly tripped over a corpse with his back leaning against the rear wheel, clothes on fire, and lying huddled up like a scarecrow of straw. The air stank of explosive.

At one of the front windows sat a medical orderly, leaning against the broken sill and staring into the road. I ran up and asked him if he had seen any troops. He nodded and pointed up the street.

I saw Major M ---'s face staring over a pile of rubble about fifty yards distant. Some one began firing down the street. I dashed across and sprawled down between him and Johnny A ----, who was the section staff sergeant of the other flight.

"What's the news?"

"Our section's wiped out, sir."

"Didn't you get my runner? I sent him over to say we were pulling back."

"I saw someone run up. He ran smack into a grenade."

We lay flat for two or three minutes until the firing ceased. Major M --- gave me another grenade and a bandolier. We scrambled up and ran for cover behind the Field Hospital in the shuttered house. Two young Dutchmen with orange armbands were crouched against the back wall. They asked us whether the Germans were coming. Major M ---- pointed towards the street: then he cursed himself for telling them, thinking they might be spies.

We ran across the back garden and down a path beside a row of yew trees. On our right lay a thicket: behind it stood a tall, grey house with a terreted roof.

"That's Div. H.Q."

At the end of the row of yews we met a sentry from "B" squadron. Major M --- asked him where he could find the colonel; the sentry pointed down the path beside the house. We walked past a row of trenches dug at the side of the path until we came to a wide clearing. The path was bordered by a row of young oaks: on the left lay an allotment that extended to a street bordered on the far side by private houses: on the right stood a green pavilion and a cinder running track encircling an expanse of grass. Beyond the track lay a hard tennis court enclosed by a high fence of wire netting: a group of about sixty German prisoners were squatting at one end: six or seven others were slouching round the walls of their cage.

By the pavilion we met four survivors of our own flight, including Sergeant H ---, the man who had shot the grenade thrower in the stomach. We lay in a line in a dry ditch by the side of the path and each one recounted his story of the attack. When we had finished, Major M --- made a list of the known casualties.

Enemy mortar shells were landing on the allotment. We began to dig. We had only three excavating tools between us and were compelled to work in shifts. The earth in the ditch was mixed with broken glass and pottery, garbage, and old tins that still retained their smell.

At midday, Major M --- departed for Divisional H.Q., after conferring with the colonel and the major commanding "B" squadron. He told us to wait where we were, excepting Johnny A ----, who went with him.

We borrowed another spade and continued digging. When I sat down for the first rest I felt a strange tingling sensation, half relief, half exultation, when I remembered the morning's escape. I was angry at having been compelled to run: but confident now that I had survived the baptism of fire.

While we were working an officer came down the path and gave us some news. It was rather serious. The paratroops at the bridge had been isolated from the rest of the Division. We were hard pressed by large German reinforcements that had been mustered from a wide area during the last three days. The Division was falling back and concentrating in a horseshoe shaped perimeter surrounding the headquarters, with its base on the river bank a mile south of where we were standing. The Second Army had passed through Nijmegen, but they were held by heavy German fire on the road between the two rivers.

In the afternoon we began to hunger and thirst as a result of the frantic digging of the morning. I entered the pavilion and searched the empty rooms: they were littered with broken glasses and bottles and straw. Behind the changing room was a little kitchen with an electric cooker standing against one wall. By some stroke of good fortune it was still working, and two of the squadron pilots were making some coffee. When they had finished I borrowed their saucepan and brewed some for our party in a china pot that I unearthed from the cupboard.

I found some cups lying among the straw and carried the coffee back to our trenches. We sat on the slope of the bank and sipped a cup in turn, while we watched the prisoners pacing up and down inside the tennis court. The coffee did not slake our thirst, so H --- collected some bottles from the pavilion and walked down to a well at the end of the path.

Jimmy T ----, who occupied the next trench to mine, produced a glass jar filled with preserved carrots. He had scrounged it from a ration party returning from a foraging mission. We passed the jar from hand to hand and each grabbed a fistful. The carrots were floating in sweetened water, which increased our thirst.

In the middle of the afternoon we saw another supply drop from the R.A.F. They flew over as usual, wave after wave through the flak. The containers thumped down on to the allotment and the running track. Half of the planes were flying wide of the zone and a sentry who stood in the centre of the grass fired a stream of Verey cartridges into the air in a frantic attempt to indicate our position. We could see only a small section of the whole formation. I saw none hit from where we stood, but many must have fallen.

Before it grew dark I collected the glass bottles and made a visit to the well. It was built at the side of a farmhouse. An old Dutchman stood at the door talking to some paratroops. A young girl was standing by the well.

After dark the mortar fire became more intense. One shell struck the concrete foundation of the pavilion and shattered the remaining window. At midnight it grew very cold: I dragged a tarpaulin from the kitchen and sat in the trench with the folds wrapped round my shoulders. At two o'clock I had my first hour of sleep.

DAY 5
Thursday 21st September, 1944

At dawn they expected an attack. A patrol was sent across the allotment to search the gardens on the far side of the street. We lay in wait, peering over the crest of the bank. A man dragged a PIAT into a gap in the hedge and was joined by the number two carrying a load of bombs.

The morning sun rose, but the attack never came. I began to clear the bottom of my trench, hacking away the root of a tree that had jabbed into my back in the night. When I folded the tarpaulin and placed it to one side I noticed a bloodstain on the corner. It had been used as part of a stretcher the day before.

We were visited by the squadron sergeant major, a tall, thin-faced Scotsman, who had been my drill instructor at the depot two years before. I remembered my first drill parade, when I had been deafened by a barrage of orders to "March ! Halt ! March ! About turn ! To the front, salute !" He was now as cheerful as a cricket, walking round with a whole armoury of pistols strapped to his sides. He stood in the path and chatted about Scotland, football, and the merits and de-merits of Sir Harry Lauder. He survived the next five days, but three months later he was killed in a plane crash in the Pyrenees.

For breakfast we shared a ration with another section. While we were eating, one of the paratroop sentries escorted a girl prisoner up to the latrine door at the back of the pavilion. She was an ugly girl, with a snub nose and sunken eyes: she had been working at a telephone exchange in one of the barracks. We were not impressed.

At ten o'clock we heard news that our squadron had returned to the wood where we had waited on Tuesday, beside the cottage with the rabbit hutch and the rows of cabbages. We crammed the remainder of the biscuit ration in our pockets. We filched some empty bottles from the pavilion kitchen and filled them from the well. Then we moved off down the path towards Division H.Q.

As we passed the building a heavy mortar barrage fell on the roof and in the garden. We flattened ourselves in the trough of a flower-bed and waited until it had subsided. When the barrage had lifted I saw the Div. Commander walk down the steps and survey the damage. He looked like an outraged householder whose roses had been ravaged by a gang of street dogs. He was a tall, dark man with a pale face and black moustache.

On the far side the garden of the H.Q. was bordered by the main road. We ran across the stone cobbles and tram lines and dashed into some laurels that fenced a garden. Some more shells fell behind us on the H.Q.

When we arrived at the cottage we saw that its roof had been badly shattered and the walls chipped by splinters. The garden was strewn with furniture belonging to the family: they had all disappeared. Major M --- was sitting in the garden beside a cooking fire, talking to the sergeant major. We reported to him and were dispatched to fill some empty trenches that had been dug beneath the hedge.

I chose a deep hole that required no further digging. After dumping my kit I looked round to see if there was anyone I knew. The squadron had lost nearly half its men: out of our section only H --- and myself remained.

A few minutes later the party of us that had just arrived were recalled to the cottage. The sergeant major told us to report to Captain P ---- at a position a hundred yards westwards along the edge of the wood. We were given some new entrenching tools to replace those we had lost in our flight the day before.

When we met Captain P --- he told us to dig a defensive position among the roots of a group of beeches, facing down a path that led towards the centre of the wood. It was a hazardous place for a defence: as far as one could see a dense growth of holly and young fir trees screened the trunks of the taller trees. Our kneeling shapes could be seen clearly by anyone who approached from the enemy side.

We hacked away at the roots for an hour without rest. We were joined by a paratroop sergeant whose platoon had been wiped out and by two other paratroops who were carrying a Vickers gun. They mounted the gun in a narrow gap between two trunks and stacked the ammunition in the ditch at the wood's edge.

On our left flank, further to the south, a company of the Borderers were clearing an area of the wood. Throughout the morning we heard almost continuous firing and the shouting of orders.

Captain P ---- gave us a summary of the course of the battle. Our squadron position formed the northwest corner of a defensive perimeter. The division had fallen back to within this area on the previous day, when the tide of battle had turned and we were forced on the defensive. For the first time our prospects seemed not too bright. In the first three days the paratroop battalions had been nearly annihilated after their attacks to clear a way towards the town bridge.

At midday we had dug fairly deep, so we decided to rest for a meal. The sergeant major sent us a sackful of rations holding some tinned Maconochies and plum pudding. I scrambled down into a nearby gravel pit, where I lit a fire and heated the tins among the burning sticks.

In the afternoon the firing quietened down. We were told to expect an attack at any moment. There were strange cries in the wood: some of them sounded German. At three o'clock we were warned that the Borderers would be clearing the ground to our front: we were told to hold our fire unless we saw a German in full view.

In the evening the assault came. A few yards to the right, in a thicket of small firs, we heard a whistle and an order shouted in German. Our Bren gunner fired a burst. Someone in the thicket screamed at the top of his voice. The sergeant major, who could speak German, stood up behind a tree and called out an order. A grey clad figure stood up in a clump of bushes and raised his hands. Just at that moment one of us fired his rifle at a sudden movement on our left. The German dived back into cover. The sergeant major shouted another order. No one answered.

We were joined by Major M ---. He and the sergeant major walked up to the edge of the firs and continued shouting: "Coomen zee hier ! Rouscommen ! " The attackers remained silent. We charged into the trees with fixed bayonets and fired into the screen of branches. There was much shouting and firing; we found ourselves in the centre of two German sections who were retreating hastily into the wood. I crashed through some trees and stumbled full length into a sandpit about ten feet square and two feet deep. There were three wounded Germans lying in the bottom. Our paratroop sergeant was bandaging the leg of one, while Johnny A --- stuffed a cigarette between the German's lips and gave him a light. He was lying beside a machine gun and several boxes of ammunition. A few paces past the pit were two dead privates and an officer, who still wore a pair of spectacles as thick as burning glass.

At this moment our counter attack was called back. Our foremost file had walked into the line of a Vickers gun firing across our front. Major M ---- staggered back with a wound on the neck, leaning on the shoulder of one of our pilots and looking very green in the face. He was taken away to the hospital and Captain P ---- took command. We carried back the machine gun, its ammunition, five or six German rifles, and a batch of prisoners.

That evening our padre arranged an hour's truce with the enemy, so that both sides could collect their dead and wounded who were lying in the wood. The Borderers had lost many men in the clearing operation and the paths and bushes were littered with dead Germans. We saw by their tunic markings and the skull-shaped badge on their caps that they were S.S. troops. A German M.O. came to our command post to arrange the truce. While he was standing near, one of our officers commented on the danger of security in allowing him to enter, and suggested that the truce might be broken by the enemy.

The M.O. turned on him in indignation and said: "Zee Germans doo not break zare vord!"

So far as our own experience taught us, this was perfectly true. They were very particular in such matters of etiquette and were chivalrous to our wounded.

At nightfall we were relieved by another section. I went back near the cottage and installed myself in a deep hole back near the cottage that had been dug to protect some ammunition. It was very spacious, about six feet square and five feet deep. I shared it with a young second pilot who I discovered sitting in one corner holding a jar of preserved cherries that he had unearthed from the cottage cellar. Before very long the bottle was empty.

DAY 6
Friday 22nd September, 1944

Throughout the night we kept watch in turn. During my period of rest I wrapped myself in the silk of a parachute in an attempt to keep warm. Although I had remained almost continuously awake during the previous five days, I slept only fitfully. I had some queer dreams. They were all unconnected with the events of the moment. I remember a distorted vision of our old crew room at the aerodrome; a row of ferns in a restaurant where I used to eat before the war; and an embarrassing scene that had no foundation in my previous life, when I walked into the cloakroom of a Y.M.C.A. and discovered that the second initial was really a "W". There may be some Freudian explanation for the last dream – as yet I have not been informed.

At dawn a general stand-to was ordered. We expected another attack, but the woods remained silent and the first mortar fire did not fall until ten o'clock.

Captain P --- walked round the trenches, asked how we were and told us some news. The Second Army was still held on the single road from Nijmegen to Arnhem, though heavy reinforcements were expected. He assured us that we would be relieved in a day or two, but all of us doubted this. We had heard too many rumours in the last few days.

In the action of the previous day I had taken a water bottle from the belt of a dead German to replace the one I lost on Wednesday. After a breakfast of biscuits and some boiled sweets we needed some water for the tea.

I made a journey to a house across the street from the cottage, where the main had not been cut. We had marched down this street on the Tuesday evening when we passed the windows filled with waving hands. It was now desolate. The tiles were smashed by mortar fire and the windows gaping. The families had either left or were hiding in the cellars, from which they only emerged to draw water or borrow supplies of food from their neighbours. The ground and upper floors were occupied by pickets of our own men: some from my regiment and some from the K.O.S.B.s

As I crossed the street some shells whizzed overhead on the way to Div. H.Q. I ran to the door and knocked loudly, eager to enter in case the next salvo fell short. A face peered round the door and I recognized Bill R --- whom I had known in training days. He looked pale and unshaven and shaken. His squadron had suffered a grim setback two days before when they had been surrounded and forced to fight their way through a ring of Germans, losing half their men. He led me upstairs to the bathroom where I drew the water from a chipped bath with a thick layer of sand along the bottom. This sand impregnated our tea and remained in a thin coating on our tongues and behind our teeth.

In the morning my section were given a rest from active patrolling and told to stand guard in the trenches by the cottage garden. I shared a watch with Sergeant -------. During my rests I read a copy of the Daily Express of the previous day's edition that had been dropped in one of the ammunition containers on that date. The headlines were optimistic. They announced that "Dempsey Does It Again" referring to an armoured column that had survived from Nijmegen into Germany. There were several broad black arrows on the map pointing in our direction, and the relief of our position was prophesied to occur within a few hours, or perhaps a day.

A few moments after I had read these lines I overheard Captain P ---- speaking to the sergeant major. He told him that he had just attended a brigade commanders' conference, where our prospects of relief had been revealed. The division had been almost halved in numbers and ammunition was very short. The Div. Commander had warned the Second Army by wireless that we might be over-run within forty-eight hours.

In the afternoon we were worried by snipers, who killed or wounded several men in our outpost trenches. On the east of the cottage there was a circular ditch or fosse encircling a high mound on which was built a little mausoleum of stone. It was enclosed in the wood and screened from sight by rows of pines and young beeches that grew up to the walls. Our outposts were dug all round the eastern half of the circle, where their snipers could approach within a few yards. Further damage was incurred by an assault gun that fired from a nearby bridge, aiming at the tree tops; the shells splintered into fragments that were deflected downwards into our foxholes.

At six o'clock the enemy staged a further attack. We heard several blasts on a whistle and some machine-gun bullets sprayed the northern hedge. My section was called out from their position by the cottage to man some empty trenches in the sector of the assault. A section of S.S. made a frontal assault through a thicket of young pines. The two foremost men had passed between two of our trenches before they fell with bullets in the stomach. There was some further shouting in the bushes further back, but the attack was pressed with little vigour. We killed three or four more: two came forward with upstretched hands and surrendered. The remainder fell back.

We were too busy to think of removing the fallen men, and in the following days the mortar fire grew too intense. They were left to lie on the pine-needles, huddled in grotesque shapes like lay figures in a studio.

Just before nightfall I was stationed in a trench on the outer line of defence, covering a strip of path that led into the wood. The trench was very shallow and I dug a further two feet before I thought of resting.

Through the night I arranged a turn of watch with the man in the adjoining trench. At twelve o'clock it began to rain: my clothes were soon soaked through and I became too cold to sleep. I remembered that Saturday was my birthday.

That night a huge force of bombers flew past above our heads. They created a continuous thunder in the sky for the interval of an hour. I heard later that it was a raid of Lancasters on Duisberg.

The rain pattered down through the leaves and lasted through the morning.

DAY 7
Saturday 23rd September, 1944

....

We stood to at dawn. I was visited by Captain P ---. He stumbled round through the bushes from trench to trench, counting our arms and ammunition and assuring himself that we were all awake. He seemed shaky and excitable and impressed with the notion that our morale was low and required boosting. He told us that if we hung on for two or three days all would be well. As it was, our mood was more stolid and unconcerned than his.

For breakfast we were issued with a bar of chocolate. I boiled some tea in a cracked mess tin and shared it with Sergeant B ---, who rewarded me with two buttered biscuits that had been lying in the rain throughout the night.

At ten o'clock we were attacked on the northern bridge. This was the site where Gordon and I had built our trenches on the Tuesday. My position now lay several yards within the wood and I took no share in the repulse. Our line at this point was well armed; we had two six-pounders at either end of the hedge and a Vickers between. They had a wide field of fire over the ploughed field where the gun battery had once stood – now blown to extinction.

The first warning came when the assault guns began blasting a row of fir trees above the heads of the gun crews and riflemen along the hedge. The ground soon became littered with broken boughs and the trunks were seared with white scars. Three or four casualties were taken away to the roadside. Then I heard a series of whistles from across the field. The Vickers opened up with a long burst and one of the six-pounders fired. There was little difference between the deafening crack from the charge of our guns and the close-range fire of the S.P. The attack fell back.

They made five assaults in the rain and mist of the morning, but all were repulsed. One time an assault gun crawled half-way across the open field before it was smashed by two successive shells from the six-pounders: it stood scorched and derelict, poised on the edge of an old gun pit, with its dead crew sprawled behind the shield.

At twelve o'clock the rain stopped. My clothes and rifle were smeared with wet sand. When the last attack had fallen back, I sat down in the bottom of the trench and cleaned as much of the rifle as I could with a strip of parachute silk. I lit the Tommy cooker and brewed the remainder of my tea ration.

I was joined by two privates from the K.O.S.B.s. They were part of a platoon that were regrouping in our lines before making a counter attack across the field into the copse on the further side. As is so often the case in British regiments, neither of them came from the area where their unit was founded; one had been a Durham coal miner, the other a shop assistant in Leicester. The latter was a stocky youth with a hooked nose and lined face, old for his years. He was very talkative and described to me the terrific mortar barrage his company had suffered the day before. The casualties among the K.O.S.B. were appalling: only one man in ten survived the operation.

We shared the last of our cigarettes and chocolate and they helped me to deepen my trench. At one o'clock they were taken away by their platoon commander, who spoke with a Canadian accent.

For the remainder of the day we were spared a further assault. The weather cleared, our clothes dried and our spirits were cheered. We heard further rumours of a contact with the Second Army. Some shells that whizzed overhead from south to north, an unusual direction, were reported to be British. The morning battle had given us new confidence.

There had been no re-supply by air for the last two days. We were told that the weather and the size of our perimeter had prevented the accurate dropping of the containers. For all this, the sky was filled with British fighters, the Typhoons and Thunderbolts were strafing the enemy lines with salvoes of rocket shells. They would swing down in an almost vertical dive; the rockets were ejected with a harsh, searing sound like a steel-cutting saw. They burst in clumps behind the roof tops, in the streets beyond the field.

In the afternoon the group of pilots who were entrenched beside the path, were organised into a defense section under the leadership of Lieut. C ---. We expected a counter attack through the cover of the wood, and two Brens were brought up from squadron H.Q.

Lieut. C --- was a hefty, dark-haired officer with a bristling moustache and a rather piratical Corsican air. I remembered him in the role of censoring officer at one of our aerodromes in England, where his naïve manner was rather intriguing. He had a brusque but hearty manner of speaking. In our presence he would read our mail with evident relish, nodding, scowling, or laughing at the different passages as if the letters were addressed to himself. In the capacity of section officer he displayed as much gusto as if he were just promoted to command of a company, and hopped around the position ordering the re-siting of Brens and riflemen. He collected our ration of chocolate and biscuits for the following day: a useful measure when the supply conditions had been reduced to near chaos by the heavy mortar shelling along the street.

At dark we received a hurried visit from the Adjutant. He had assumed command of the squadron when Captain P ----- had been wounded in the leg at midday. He reported that he had been nearly struck by a sniper's bullet while he was ambling up the path towards our trenches, and asked C

----- to send out a patrol of two or three men into the screen of undergrowth on the west of the path. Three of us were told to scour the bushes in this direction. I had only taken a few paces past the track when I nearly stumbled over the body of Lieut. A ----, our intelligence officer who had been shot on the previous evening. I decided to crawl for the rest of the way. It was lucky that I did.

A few seconds later I saw a section of Germans stalking round the wreckage of a container, attached by its tangled cords to a red parachute entangled in the trees. They were armed only with rifles, so I hid behind the trunk of an oak and took a shot at the leader. He shouted, grabbed his upper arm and crouched behind the container. The remainder scattered. I reloaded, but the bolt jammed and I crawled away hastily to another tree trunk.

I waited for two or three minutes, but the Germans did not reappear. I crawled back to the section by a circular route and discovered the body of Sergeant B ----, whom I had known at home, lying face downwards in the leaves. I remember noticing his boots were newly soled, with rows of steel studs still shining from recent wear. When I returned to the foxhole I met Tommy M ----, who formerly had shared the same tent in North Africa. The mortaring had ceased for an interval and we were able to stand and chat for a few minutes.

Soon afterwards we arranged our watches and settled down for the night. My first turn was from eleven to one.

The sky was much clearer that on Friday night and patterned with stars. During the day I had cut some pine branches from the young trees at the side and laid them on the floor of the hole to form a couch. They exuded a strong resinous scent that became more apparent in the night.

DAY 8
Sunday 24th September, 1944

At one o'clock I was startled by a rustle in the trees across the path. I remembered the German patrols of the evening and the danger of snipers: it was probable that their activities had continued throughout the night. Cocking the rifle, I placed a Mills bomb ready and listened. The rustling renewed and I began to visualise the presence of several men, perhaps forming up for an attack.

A few yards distant a twig crackled. I gave the first half of the password, but no one answered. I saw a vague grey movement in the blackness of a fir, aimed – and fired. The trigger clicked, but there was no report. The round was a dud. As I re-cocked, a voice asked: "What the hell's the matter?" It was Sergeant -----, who had been holding a forward foxhole to our front on the edge of the ditch. He had been relieved two minutes before and had lost his direction in the wood, while he stumbled back to H.Q. My voice sounded further away than it actually was: some acoustic freak caused by the screen of damp leaves and trunks. He had assumed I challenged another man and failed to answer until he heard the click of the pin. Back at camp he still accused me of attempted murder!

There were no further incidents that night. At the end of my watch I had two hours sleep, returning to my post an hour before dawn. For the first few hours of day we were left in peace. The mortar fire was directed over our heads in the direction of Div. H.Q. the "hotspot" of the whole bridgehead. Our ammunition was re-sorted, the rations checked, the trenches were deepened. Captain D --- -- walked round the positions and re-arranged the sections so that more men were placed on the sector of our position that faced into the wood. An attack through the thick cover of beech and oak saplings was anticipated.

As a fighting unit the squadron was a most conglomerate force. It was formed from the remnants of ---- and ----- squadrons. There were two six-pounders and their crews from the Border regiment, in the hedge was a Vickers gun manned by two parachutists and in the slit trenches by the mound were several men from the other squadrons. We wore an odd assortment of garments, especially our headgear. Johnny M ---- wore an American helmet, Dick ----, a Dutch cap that he had picked up from the railway, several wore scarves of parachute silk and green and brown camouflage nets knotted round their heads.

Late in the morning we experienced a sudden surprise. There was a rumble of tracked wheels down the drive on the further side of the mausoleum and the "toc-toc-toc" of a heavy machine gun. I heard our flank section return the fire. A moment later I saw a series of flashes through the leaves, or rather the blurred reflection, like sheet lightening hidden by a heavy screen of cloud. Any further noise from that direction was drowned for the moment due to the screeching of another barrage of shells, destined for Div. H.Q. When this subsided, the machine-gun fire had become subdued. There were two or three blasts sounded on a whistle and the firing ceased.

From my position I could not realise what had happened, but on the following day I learnt that the southern section, entrenched in the position where we captured the two Spandaus, had been attacked by a flame throwing tank. The section had been pushed back, leaving two of my friends sprawling in their holes, burned to death. For some inexplicable reason the tank had turned back at the end of the line, and had trundled off into the wood.

Several of these flame-throwing tanks had been prowling around the outside of the division's perimeter during the preceding days, but this was the only occasion on which our sector was attacked. These and the assault guns were the most formidable threat to our defences, for the infantry attacks by the S.S. were ill-timed and undetermined and always announced beforehand by the usual whistles and gutteral shouting.

In the afternoon we had a respite. We sat in the trenches and watched two or three waves of Typhoons and Thunderbolts dive overhead to strafe the enemy positions behind the houses of a nearby street. I pulled my rifle to pieces and cleaned off the damp sand. While I was cutting some new pine branches from the copse, I discovered the body of Lieut. ----, our intelligence officer, who had been killed in the attack of Friday evening. He was lying face downwards with his head buried in a clump of heather, his arms bent stiffly on the ground before him, as if he had been crawling. There was another body, of a young German corporal, lying half on his side, with the knapsack that was strapped to his belt gaping open, revealing a damp lump of brown bread and a rusty knife. I felt hungry enough to eat the bread. When I touched it, it felt like damp rubber, so I let it lie.

Soon after I returned to the trench with the pine branches, I heard someone shouting in German from the wood. I went back to the larch trunk from where I had fired at a previous patrol. I saw some rustling in the bushes and heard a few whispers. I ran back and warned Lieut C ----, the pirate with the black moustache. He led a patrol of three men and himself in that direction: we discovered nothing so the others must have shied away.

At five o'clock we gathered rations at the "Pirate's" trench. He seemed in a cheerful mood and we began exchanging jokes about our present situation. Someone with a rather saturnine sense of humour, compared it to a game of musical chairs.

When I returned to my foxhole with the rations, I stacked them on the side and jumped down into the bottom to reach for the cooking stove. As my feet touched the sand there was a sudden tremendous report. I felt a sharp jab at my side and was flung to my knees. The rations were blown into the trench on top of my back. The air was filled with flying sand and smoke. A branch and some wood splinters tumbled down from the trunk of a pine. Then, seconds later there was another report, followed by more sand and splinters and smoke. I ducked down and squatted in the corner of the trench. There was a trickle of water running down my hip. I looked down and saw that the top half of the German water bottle I had been wearing had been shattered by a piece of shrapnel from the first explosion. It lay in the sand at my foot, still warm from the burst.

The explosions continued at nine or ten second intervals. I realised that some gun at very close range was firing shells at the crest of the trees and the splinters were deflected vertically downwards. I also realized how victims contract shell-shock. The crack of the explosions was shaking the walls of the trench and beating against my head. When a third splinter had smacked into the sand beside me, I reckoned it was time to shift my station to another trench. The German gun-layer had too strong a fancy for the trees above my particular head. I waited for the next shell to burst, then grabbed my rifle and sling and made a hop, skip, and jump into another trench about ten yards away. It was occupied by a sergeant from the other squadron whose face I did not recognise. He mumbled some conventional epithet about the temperature of our surroundings. The next burst brought a splinter that tore a great hole in his back. I could see the jagged vent in his smock. He gave a scream and slumped into the corner of the pit. I shook him by the shoulder. He mumbled a few words and then died.

I moved into another trench a little to the left. The shelling ceased after two or three more rounds. After a few minutes we were ordered to withdraw to the command post, where Captain P ---- was in charge. The casualties were counted and proved very heavy. As we were standing in the garden, sorting the bandoliers and remaining brens, the shelling began again. Captain P --- ordered a withdrawal to the row of houses across the street.

We dashed across in turn by small groups. I found myself in the back room of a little thatched house, with bricked walls and latticed windows. It was very trim, like a weekend cottage at Selsey Bill. The room presented a tangled chaos of curtains, sofas, armchairs, chintz-covered cushions, ammunition boxes, rifles, webbing equipment, and the remains of a meal scattered over the pile carpet. It was already occupied by four members of another flight, who had commandeered it two days before. The scattered food, the torn rugs, the pile of chairs, and the bureau jammed into the bay window were evidence enough.

I recognized old Tim M ---, whom I had last seen on the further side of a table in a Leicester café during a weekend leave. He looked very white, but still managed to grin. He was killed on the following day.

Within five minutes the remnants of the squadron had been withdrawn from the wood. Two or three parties returned to retrieve a box or two of ammunition and to dispatch the wounded on to a jeep for the Div. Hospital up the street. Captain P --- walked through the houses and arranged a plan for defence. There were found to be too many people in the thatched cottage, so Nellie and I were moved to the next house. We found ourselves among a group of eight men. There was Nellie B ----, who was a Yorkshireman, myself, and four Borderers and two second pilots. The house had not been occupied by our troops and remained in a tidy condition. The Dutch family were still in residence, down in the cellar. We could hear their voices through the floor as we stumbled about the house, piling the furniture against the windows. Nellie assumed command. He placed the Borderers upstairs, while the remainder stayed on the ground floor. We arranged a tour of sentry for the night, with one man guarding the street window and the other watching the garden.

We expected an attack from our old position in the wood, but the enemy had not moved. For all we knew he had not learned of our withdrawal. He may have feared our two six-pounders. One of them lay shattered in its pit, the other had been moved to the garden at the corner of the street.

In a short while the sun had set. Nellie took the first shift at the front window. I lay down in a corner and wrapped myself in a curtain and a rug, with a fur mat for a pillow. I felt cold and very tired after seven nights of almost ceaseless watch.

"The boat's head began to swing down-stream"

DAY 9
Monday 25th September, 1944

The sky was cloudy, but a little light from a new moon filtered through the mist and whitened the expanse of road beyond the garden railing. Across the road to the north stood the house where we had drawn water during the last few days. Away to the left the road ended at the corner by the wood, opposite the little cottage with the vegetable garden and the rabbits. To the right, the file of houses faded into the darkness towards the park. Beyond the opposite houses I could see the glow of a big fire from a further street on the edge of the German lines. Throughout the night there was very little sound except for some distant firing.

Each time that Nellie woke me for a spell of watch, I felt colder and more depressed. Our withdrawal from the wood after standing firm for five days had come as a sudden shock. It had seemed that we would hold for ever.

In the early morning I went into the kitchen to make some tea. The gas and water supply had been cut, but I found a few gallons of water in the bath, that had a gritty taste, and I used the last of my fuel tablets on the toasting tray beneath the gas ring. The hot tea soon warmed our limbs and cheered our spirits.

In the hall I found a discarded rucksack that no one claimed. It contained soap and a towel. I explored the upper floor and found a washbowl and a mirror. The first sight of my own face after seven days was a little disconcerting. I had grown a heavy stubble of beard, stained yellow from the sand of my trench. The remainder of my skin was a sickly grey colour, probably caused by lack of sleep and a mixed diet of condensed rations and preserved fruit. I washed off a large proportion of the sand and made a brave attempt to comb my hair.

At seven o'clock we were visited by two from the family below. There was a young man of about twenty-five who brought up a saucepan of vegetables and a pile of wood. He lit the stove in the back room, talked to us the whole while in Dutch, which none of us understood. He was followed by a smaller, dark man of about the same age, probably his brother. The latter could speak a few words of English. He told us that his parents, his sister-in-law and her four-year-old child were also living below. They had moved to the cellar after the heavy bombardment on the Wednesday morning, when most of the windows in the street had been shattered and many of the tiles removed.

The dark-haired brother gave us a saucepan of potatoes which we put aside in one corner for use at midday. They returned down the stairs to the cellar.

A little later I decided to visit Wing H.Q. to ask for some information. On the evening before, I had discovered that it was situated in a large brick house in a garden on the further side of our back fence. I climbed out through the broken French windows of the back room, ran across the lawn, and stumbled over the wires. It was necessary to move in short bursts, for we had heard the neighbourhood was filled with snipers. I reached the backyard of the house and looked in at the garage door. The place was empty except for a pile of timber in one corner and a bloodstained body lying in the middle of the floor beneath a sheet.

I had expected the house to be filled with people, but for a few moments I found no trace of occupation. Then I heard a sound of voices from the upper floor. A sentry with a rifle clambered down the stairs and asked me what I wanted. I asked him for news: he directed me down to the cellar. There I found a group of five pilots around the floor on a pile of bedding, army blankets, dirty shirts, and an eiderdown taken from the bedroom.

Most of them were flight sergeants who had reported to the H.Q. on the same errand as myself. I recognised Johnny A ----, who had been in my flight during our stay in the wood. None of them could give me news, for Captain P ---- was still away at a Divisional conference.

When I had crawled back across the fence I decided to visit the next house to ours, to learn the number of men who held it and to meet anyone I knew. The houses in the street were semi-detached; in case of a break through by the enemy, each pair might be held as a strongpoint if a little co-operation were used.

In the back room I found Jonah and Ginger sitting against the wall, drinking tea and eating apples. Jonah was a dark, urbane, rather smooth-tongued individual whom I had known since I joined the regiment. I remember him for his ability in arguing with equal facility on both sides of a debate. All that I recollect of Ginger is that he was tall and pink-faced and was Jonah's second pilot. They gave me a share of the tea and apples while we made our estimate of our strength and ammunition.

When I returned to the room next door I encountered a minor domestic crisis. The old lady of the house had ascended from the cellar for a morning inspection. She had discovered a group of four bearded and begrimed soldiers, peeling a bucketful of potatoes in the middle of the drawing room carpet. The shattered condition of the windows and furniture had induced a lackadaisical attitude towards those that remained intact, and the group of four seemed a little disconcerted by the flow of expletives that could be heard from the garden fence. We finally calmed her feeling by offering to sweep the ground floor rooms and removing the bucket to the kitchen. Later we were visited by the old father, who withdrew some valuable china from a corner cupboard and removed a valuable old engraving of an East Indian village, conveying them to the safer recesses of the cellar.

We sat down to lunch in the middle of the afternoon. Some biscuits were found in the discarded rucksack and some boiled sweets. We mixed them with the boiled potatoes and ate from the earthenware dishes that had been left in the kitchen cupboard.

The room was suddenly shaken by a tremendous blast. The remaining glass blew in from the French window, and for a moment we were blinded by a cloud of black smoke that filled the room with fumes. As the smoke cleared I saw the dim figures of others, crouched against the walls, their plates still couched between their knees, all staring at the window. A second later three of us had crowded to the window. In the gravel patch between the glass and the lawn, there gaped a shallow hole, the size of a washbasin, lined with black powder. The German mortars had returned.

During the following hour several bombs fell within the street, and one hit the corner wall of the neighbouring house. We returned to our stations at the window ledges and watched the street. There seemed a more than usual bustle among the houses on the further side. We were visited by Tommy M ----, who had been appointed as Lieutenant to Captain P ----. He asked Nellie B --- to accompany him to Wing H.Q.

When Nellie returned, he wore a very secretive expression. He asked us whether the Dutch family were all downstairs and nosed around the staircase door to assure himself they were. Then he closed the door of the room upon us, crouched down in a corner and spoke in a low murmur.

"I don't want anyone else to hear this. We're pulling out tonight, over the river. The Second Army can't cross. We lost the bridge several days ago and our tanks can't pass their guns to reach it. They've got some officers of the ----, who came in last night. The Dorsets are going to hold a bridgehead tonight on our bank while we cross."

There were more details that he gave us. We were to assemble on a little patch of grass behind the garden at nine-fifteen; we were to bring any surplus kit; we were to cover our boots with strips of blanket and rug cut from those in the room; we were to follow white tapes down to the river; we were to retain our arms at any price; we should keep together.

Our first reaction to this news was one of dazed surprise, almost shock. For nine days we had held one belief; the Second Army was coming through. We had heard rumours and more rumours of their steady advance to the river bank, of vast lines of tanks on the Nijmegen road, of lines of guns firing a barrage over our heads. When the shell had burst through our window that afternoon we had assumed it might be British, for the blast had blown from south to north, and from the south we expected the British. At four o'clock we had watched a sortie of Typhoons swooping down on the German lines to the north, heard the rasping and booming of their rocket fusillade and seen them return above the street unopposed. The enemy had made no attack, and the situation we had thought, relieved.

Nellie had to answer a barrage of questions. Someone in the corner began a heated argument. We heard the cellar door bang and the voices of the young Dutchman and his wife. Our talking ceased.

The young wife entered the room and began to sort some ornamental plates on the dresser. Her husband joined her and they began a discussion, probably on the removal of the furniture. They stood beneath a huge parchment lampshade that swung from the roof, adorned with rows of beads and glass, like a bargain from Bowmans. The woman fingered with the attachments, as if she intended to dismantle it, then turned away towards the window. I offered them my cigarettes and struck a match. After a few puffs, the man grinned and asked me when the Second Army were coming.

"Oh, tomorrow, perhaps."

"You said that last week. Tomorrow, tomorrow: it's always tomorrow."

They walked out with the pile of plates.

As they disappeared down the stairs, one of the K.O.S.B's came from across the street. He brought a message from the colonel of his battalion, whose H.Q. lay in a house near the corner, asking for a patrol of four men to report to him at once. Nellie sent Stan T ----, and two Borderers men and myself.

We ran across the road and through the front gardens to the side door of the H.Q. The colonel was standing in the kitchen. He was a short, plump person with a hooked nose and sandy moustache. He was dressed in a helmet and smock with the badges of rank ripped from the shoulders. Nearly all the officers in his battalion had been killed by snipers, and he was taking no chances. His voice was hoarse and a little rumbling.

He told Stan to take charge of a patrol of twelve men, comprised of K.O.S.B.s, paratroops, Borderers, and glider pilots, and to reconnoitre the gardens of the houses in the street to the north – a section of no-man's land that we presumed the Germans had left unoccupied. We were ordered to fire on sight or sound of any suspicious movement, but should avoid any stand up fight. The purpose of the patrol was to inform the Germans that we were still active and to conceal our intention that we would withdraw that evening.

We filed out along the fence of the back garden and climbed some railings at the further end. Before us lay the ruins of the cottage that had been burning during the night. The brick walls had crumbled to within three or four feet from the ground and the open rooms were piled high with ash. We passed along the side of the wall and scanned the houses to the front. They were a row of semi-detached villas of the same design as those in our own streets. There was no sign of movement from the windows or doors. The only sound we heard was the crackling of some burning wood on the far side of the cottage, and a rustle in the bushes. Then we saw a movement there. A sergeant from the Recce corps stepped clear, rather blunderingly, his smock torn and his face black with wood ash.

"Have you seen my boys?" he asked. "I left them on guard in the cellar."

He walked past us and lumbered over the brick wall into the embers. He moved to one corner and stirred a hole in the ash with the butt of his Sten gun. He whistled and called in a low voice: "Hey, Ted ! Ted !"

Then he moved to another corner and called again. For several minutes he stumbled around the inner walls. Finally he stepped back over the outer wall and was hidden again in the bushes.

We moved on to the next garden, then turned to the right and crept through a shrubbery of currant bushes. We crouched there for a few minutes and watched the row of houses. Then Stan beckoned us to follow and we returned to H.Q. From the H.Q. garden we all dispersed our different ways.

In the tiled bath of the billet the Dutch family were gathered, silent but inquisitive. We passed by them and closed the inner door. The light was already failing and we had little time to lose in making preparation for the march to the river. Two men knelt on the floor and began cutting a blanket into narrow strips. Nellie carried the rucksack upstairs and hid it in the loft; a public burial in the garden might reveal our intentions. From the kitchen cupboard I unearthed the last clean saucepan and emptied into it the remainder of our tea ration for a final brew. By the time this had boiled, the sun had set; I stumbled down a darkened passage into the dim confusion of the back room.

We sat, huddled in separate corners and sipped the tea. Final orders were whispered round the room. Dusk turned total darkness. A few feet from my face I could see the luminous dial of Nellie's watch: it would hover in the air, then rise or fall or vanish, like some fleeting marsh light. Every few minutes he would raise his wrist and note the time. There was a movement in the passage. Someone called from the cellar stairs. We heard the stair head door slam, and steps descending. From beneath the floor we heard the sound of a child's voice, questioning and shrill. Presently there was silence.

At nine o'clock Nellie stood up before the white square of window and beckoned us to follow. Our blanket-shod feet made a dull crunch on the gravel. Apart from a few kicks against the window frame we made little sound. From the gardens on either side we could see dim lines of figures advancing in the same direction. Two hundred yards in front we saw the black mass of beech trees that lined the road we had to pass. The blackness was laced with scarlet arcs of tracer bullets, and the "toc-toc-toc" of machine guns echoed from all around. Far away to the south the lower sky glowed with a pale yellow light, and the heavy guns went on rumbling endlessly.

As we reached the open ground of the clearing, I heard a sudden dull "plop" from a Verey pistol in the wood, and a second later a flare burst into light in the sky above our heads. I sprawled onto my face. Looking to one side, I saw the clearing littered with a line of prostrate bodies, like fishes stranded on a beach. The Verey flare had set the grass on fire. Some mortar shells burst on the right edge of the clearing. The light dimmed and vanished. The line of bodies before me began to crawl forward on hands and knees.

At the far side of the clearing we entered some bushes, and we could venture to stand up. The groups of soldiers broke and mingled in such confusion that I was soon lost from our little party. A few yards further on I crossed a dark strip, harder beneath my feet, that I guessed to be the road. Someone nudged my shoulder and I recognised Stan T ---.

Together we shambled along behind a file of smock-clad figures into what appeared a path in a thick wood. Our only direction pointer was the dull glow from the south, where the river lay. Wherever the trees grew dense enough to screen the view, we had to move by instinct: the sound of guns was impossible to locate, for the woods echoed with the crash of shells and rattle of volleys.

Further on the path began to slope downhill; it became broader and we saw a strip of sky above our heads. On either side the trunks and undergrowth were swathed in flat streaks of phosphorous smoke. Presently we passed a white strip of cloth on the side of the path; another appeared, and then another. We had chosen the right path.

A minutes or two later I jolted against the back of the man in front. The column had halted. We were standing in a narrow cart track at the edge of the road: on our right side stood a high wall shielding the skeleton frame of an old fruit tree: on the left was a fence and a blurred waste of water meadow; to our front I saw the corner of a barn and the broken shaft of a factory chimney.

We shuffled forward in groups of two and three. Two officers were standing astride the path, scanning the face and clothes of each man before they allowed him to pass.

"For Christ's sake don't bunch," someone whispered.

Stan and I were jostled into a bunch of several others. We turned left through a hole in the wire and groped our way along a fence that ran southwards into the meadows by the river bank. I could see a dark strip of oily water and the outline of a dyke on the further bank. Beyond the dyke lay a stretch of sky that seemed ablaze. It was lit by the flashes of a barrage from the Second Army guns. I could not gauge their distance from us, but the whole ground seemed to shake. On either side the river was arched with streaks of tracer curling upwards from the British and German lines. The field that lay between the water and our feet was half lit by the moon; across it stretched a sinuous queue of men. One or two were standing at the river bank, but most were sitting or lying on the grass, quiet as ghosts.

Beneath the rumble of field guns on the far side and the rattle of fire in the woods at our back, I heard a faint undertone of sound, the chugging of an outboard motor on the river; the ferrying had begun. While I stood in the cover of a ditch, waiting among a long file for the order to move; I watched the moonlit queue and wondered that they should stand there unseen, when the enemy were so near. It seemed miraculous that two thousand men could cross unobserved.

I did not wonder long. There came a succession of "plop, plop, plops" from a mortar battery in the wood, and the next moment a string of shells burst in the centre of the queue. They were followed by another "crump" that landed near the ditch. There were screams and shouts for help. Several voices shouted "Scatter". Bodies crawled in all directions. An officer at the bend moved the queue about fifty yards downstream. The next "crump" of shells fell accurately on the new position. The wounded who were able to, crawled away, the others were carried by their mates. Two officers ran to the ditch and told us to push back.

"Don't bunch for Christ's sake!"

The shells began to hail down in scores. Luckily they were of small calibre and in the damp ground they burst like big squibs, and those only were hit who lay within a yard or so of their fall. The queue was moved a second time, and thinned to a narrower line.

The men were passed forward in little groups. I must have wallowed in the ditch an hour or more before our turn came. Someone called from across the field. We ran across the slope of grass and clattered on to the shelving stones of the bank. A boat was swinging against a groin of stones that sloped into the water. We waded out and heaved ourselves over the side. It was a canvas assault boat, about twenty feet long, with an outboard motor screwed to the stern. It was manned by two Canadian sappers. When the boat had filled, one of them staved off the groin with a pole and we swung into the river. The other sapper jerked the engine-starter with a rope. The engine kicked and misfired. He jerked again. The engine spluttered, chugged a few turns, then stopped. The boat swirled downstream in a fast current. We began to drift back towards the bank. The sapper cursed and began fumbling with a spare screw wrapped in paper. He bit the wrapping with his teeth. We grounded on the bank, the one we had started from.

Then a voice shouted: "Why in hell's name don't you paddle with your rifles?" The other sapper poled us into deeper water and we dipped our rifle butts in the river. An officer in the bows called the time: "In – out. In – out" The boat's head began to swing upstream. "Go slow on the port side. In – out. In – out."

We checked our downstream drift and passed mid-current. The engine started with a jolt that flung us off our balance. The bows lifted and we raced across the final reach into the shallow of the dyke. The bows grated against a stone.

F I N I S
FATEHJANG
June 1945

Staff Sergeant Ronald Gibson, who served with the
Glider Pilot Regiment in F Squadron, No. 2 Wing.

Epilogue

Although Arnhem was a victory for the Germans, with British Airborne troops forced to withdraw after failing to secure bridges across the Nederrijn (Lower Rhine), the battle is still considered to be one of the most heroic of the Second World War.

The Battle of Arnhem exacted a heavy toll on the 1st British Airborne Division but it was the Glider Pilot Regiment that suffered the highest proportion of casualties with a reduction in strength of approximately 50%. The regiment was left so badly depleted that RAF Reserve pilots were called upon to help pilot gliders for the final, large-scale Airborne Operation of the War, Operation 'Varsity'.

The Glider Pilot Regiment was disbanded in 1957 making it one of the shortest lived regiments in the history of the British army. The sheer courage and devotion to duty associated with this fine body of men earned them a level of respect and admiration that continues through to the present day.